A Great Idea
ENGINEERING

The Panama Canal

by Heather Miller

NORWOODHOUSE PRESS

COVER: A cruise ship passes through the Gatun locks on the Panama Canal.

Norwood House Press
P.O. Box 316598
Chicago, Illinois 60631

For information regarding Norwood House Press, please visit our website at:
www.norwoodhousepress.com or call 866-565-2900.

PHOTO CREDITS: Cover: © Ken Welsh/Alamy; © AP Images, 19; Bow Editorial Services, 5, 7, 24, 26, 37; © Buyenlarge/Getty Images, 15; © Classic Image/Alamy, 21; © Culver Pictures/The Art Archive at Art Resource, NY, 12; © Everett Collection Historical/Alamy, 23 ; © Jon Arnold Images Ltd/Alamy, 29, 38; © Juan Jose Rodriguez/AFP/Getty Images, 43; © Mark Eveleigh/Alamy, 40; © MPV History/Alamy, 13; © Niday Picture Library/Alamy, 6; © Rob Crandall/Alamy, 8, 9, 42; © Time Life Pictures/Getty Images, 18; © Time Life Pictures/Mansell/Getty Images, 32, 35; © Time Life Pictures/Panama Canal Photo/Getty Images, 27

LIBRARY OF CONGRESS CATALOGING-IN-PUBLICATION DATA

Miller, Heather.
  The Panama Canal / by Heather Miller.
     pages cm
  Audience: 8-12.
  Audience: Grade 4 to 6.
  Summary: "Describes the struggles and accomplishments in building the Panama Canal. Includes glossary, websites, and bibliography for further reading"-- Provided by publisher.
  Includes bibliographical references and index.
  ISBN 978-1-59953-594-4 (library edition : alk. paper)
  ISBN 978-1-60357-587-4 (ebook)
  1. Panama Canal (Panama)--Juvenile literature. I. Title.
TC774.M618 2013
627'.130972875--dc23
                                                    2013010631

Manufactured in the United States of America in North Mankato, Minnesota.
257R—032014

Contents

Note: Words that are **bolded** in the text are defined in the glossary.

Chapter 1

The Plan

The Panama Canal is a shipping shortcut. It was built by American engineers and connects the Atlantic Ocean with the Pacific Ocean. Before the canal was created, there was no way for a ship to travel easily from one side of the United States to the other.

Before the canal, ships had to sail all the way down and around the southern tip of South America. Traveling around South America was a long journey. It was

? Did You Know?
In 1520, King Charles I of Spain asked his surveyors to investigate the Isthmus of Panama as a possible canal site. They concluded it was impossible to build.

also dangerous. The waters around Cape Horn, at the southern tip of South America, were known as the sailor's graveyard.

Ships traveling from San Francisco to New York City, for example, had to sail thousands of miles. They had to go down

Before the Panama Canal, ships traveling from New York to San Francisco had to make the difficult voyage around Cape Horn, an additional 7,872 miles.

the west coast of North and South America, around Cape Horn, and then back up the east coast of South and North America. By passing through the canal, a ship saves 7,872 miles (12,669km) of travel. The canal shortens the trip by about two weeks.

More Money, Less Risk

Losing cargo and trained men at sea is tragic. Lost lives cannot be replaced. Lost ships mean lost money. By lessening the amount of money needed to move goods, shipping companies could make more money. By traveling through the Panama Canal, they could take fewer risks.

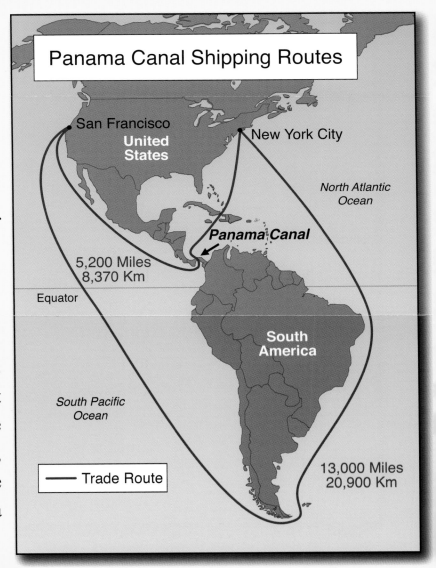

Panama Canal Shipping Routes

San Francisco

United States

New York City

North Atlantic Ocean

Panama Canal

5,200 Miles
8,370 Km

Equator

South America

South Pacific Ocean

—— Trade Route

13,000 Miles
20,900 Km

Conditions Around Cape Horn

The weather around Cape Horn is brutal. With a reported 278 days of rainfall annually (70 days of which are snow),chances of sailing around the cape on a dry day are very unlikely. Temperatures are cold and wind is high. In the winter, gale force winds occur 30 percent of the time. It is not uncommon for ships to encounter waves as tall as 100 feet (30m). The cape dips so far south that ships must look out for icebergs. Floating mountains of ice combined with high winds and freezing temperatures make Cape Horn one of the most dangerous ship passages in the world.

Isthmus Discovered

In 1513 the Spanish explorer Vasco Núñez de Balboa walked across the **Isthmus** of Panama and discovered that only a thin strip of land separated two great oceans. His discovery sparked the dream to connect the oceans. Four hundred years later, his dream became a reality when the Panama Canal was completed in 1914.

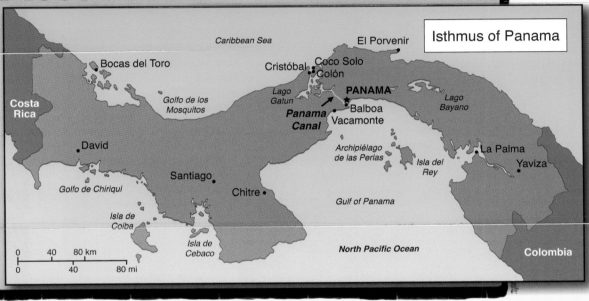

Isthmus of Panama

Caribbean Sea

Bocas del Toro

Costa Rica

Golfo de los Mosquitos

David

Golfo de Chiriqui

Isla de Coiba

Santiago

Isla de Cebaco

Chitre

Cristóbal

El Porvenir

Coco Solo

Colón

Lago Gatun

PANAMA

Panama Canal

Balboa

Vacamonte

Lago Bayano

Archipiélago de las Perlas

Isla del Rey

La Palma

Yaviza

Gulf of Panama

North Pacific Ocean

Colombia

0   40   80 km
0   40   80 mi

The Panama Canal could also increase a country's power. Using the canal as a shortcut, military ships could move quickly to different parts of the world. If only one country had control of the canal, that nation would have a military advantage over the rest of the world.

Many governments and world leaders wanted to build the Panama Canal. Many powerful people wanted a shipping

Panama's terrain is rugged, covered by thick jungles, dangerous mountain passes, and swift-running rivers.

be a fairly simple task. As far back as the 1800s, engineers had hoped to simply dig out the land and let ships pass through.

No Easy Task

The construction of the Panama Canal was not an easy task, however. Exploration and research revealed huge problems. The landscape of Panama is extremely rugged. Covered by thick jungle, the land had to be cleared before digging could begin. The isthmus also has

shortcut. When looking at a map of the Isthmus of Panama, one can see a narrow strip of land that connects two larger landmasses. A person might think that digging through the tiny strip of land would

The Chagres River was the starting point for the excavations to dig the canal. The river's strong current and destructive flooding made such a project difficult.

dangerous mountain passes. Culebra Pass, a high mountain pass of jagged, rocky cliffs, seemed to block any attempts at digging a canal across the land.

The Chagres River, which would be dug out to make the canal, was wild. High currents brought destructive floods to Panama nearly every year. Early **excavators** learned that whatever digging they did was quickly washed out or filled in by the powerful floodwaters of the Chagres.

The extreme heat of Panama made working difficult. High temperatures combined with humidity made hard, physical labor a dangerous activity. Many workers would likely die of exhaustion. The rain forests were filled with poisonous snakes and insects. Diseases like malaria and **yellow fever** were common and took the lives of many people.

A Race for Power

These problems were only the first that had to be solved. And there were even

Who Owned the Canal

Before the United States began digging the canal, Panama was controlled by Colombia. The United States helped sponsor a rebellion. With the help of US warships, Panama quickly won independence from Colombia. In return for its support, Panama gave the United States control over the Canal Zone. In 1999 the United States returned full control of the Canal Zone to Panama.

more hardships to be faced. The Panama Canal Zone was undeveloped. No towns had been established. Before construction could begin, housing, food, sewer, electricity, and drinking water systems needed to be created.

Railroad tracks also needed to be built. Trains would be used to transport both building materials and heavy machinery. A plan to create a system to carry away tons of dirt, or **spoil**, needed to be developed. Workers needed to be hired, and a chain of command would have to be established. The project was overwhelming and seemed impossible.

Despite all of these problems, the desire to create a canal across Panama was strong. The country that completed the project would have an advantage over the entire world. Owning rights to a passage that connected the Atlantic and Pacific Oceans (it also connects the Pacific to the Atlantic) meant greater power for the country that controlled the canal.

Chapter 2

Digging Begins

France was the first nation to make a serious attempt to dig the Panama Canal. After completing the Suez Canal that cuts through Egypt and connects the Mediterranean Sea to the Red Sea, the French were confident they could do it. They believed they had the knowledge and resources necessary to build a canal across Panama. Digging began in 1882.

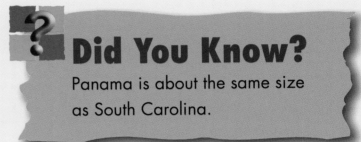

? Did You Know?

Panama is about the same size as South Carolina.

An Early Attempt Ends in Failure

French engineers planned to dig down to **sea level** across the entire isthmus. In 1881 they brought steam shovels to

The French employed Panamanian laborers to work on a diversion channel for the Obispo River in Panama. The French suffered great losses and produced little more than muddy ditches to show for their efforts.

tenth of the canal was complete. In 1889 the engineers in charge of the project quit.

By the time France gave up, more than 20,000 men had died trying to dig the canal. Millions of dollars were lost. The French were left with great losses and little more than a muddy ditch to show for their efforts. While France had struggled, the United States had watched and waited for an opportunity. After the French left Panama, the United States moved in.

Panama. They hired men who dug through mud and rock by hand.

The French faced many problems. **Rock slides** and disease killed about 350 workers each month. Heavy rains triggered mud slides that set back months of progress. By the end of 1885, only one-

Upon being appointed chief engineer of the Panama Canal project, John Wallace brought in giant steam shovels with five times the capacity of the ones used by the French.

Making Dirt Fly

Theodore Roosevelt became president of the United States in 1901. He had his sights set on Panama. He saw the failure of the French as an opportunity for the United States. In 1904 Roosevelt put engineer John Wallace in charge of the Panama Canal project. Roosevelt ordered Wallace to "make dirt fly."

Wallace wanted to spend at least one full year planning. He wanted to set up resources before starting to dig the canal. Roosevelt insisted that work begin immediately. Wallace did not have time to create a plan. He did not know how

Bucyrus Steam Shovel

The Bucyrus steam shovel was an important piece of machinery used in the construction of the Panama Canal. The company that built the shovel was founded in Bucyrus, Ohio. It moved to South Milwaukee, Wisconsin, in 1893. A proud American company, Bucyrus survived bankruptcy in 1993. It continued to operate for more than ten years. In 2011 Caterpillar purchased Bucyrus.

Historians consider the Bucyrus steam shovel to be an important part of engineering history.

Wallace ordered heavy machinery for the job. He brought in giant steam shovels built by the American company Bucyrus. The shovels were massive and powerful. Each machine weighed more than 65 tons (59t). A Bucyrus shovel could remove 4,800 cubic yards (3,670 cubic meters) of dirt and rock every eight hours. With each scoop, the steam shovel could remove 8.7 tons (7.9t) of rock. The American steam shovels could dig five times more earth than the machines used by the French.

Facing Many Setbacks

The choice to use the Bucyrus shovels was one of the only successful decisions Wallace made. As work progressed, to overcome the huge obstacles that he knew he would face.

Wallace used multiple train tracks and thousands of train cars to remove dirt and rocks from the excavation.

Wallace and his workers were faced with many problems. The Bucyrus shovels were extremely effective at removing dirt. But that meant Wallace had a new problem. He did not know how to take away the dirt that was removed by the shovels.

Railroads were built to haul the dirt away, but the cars were quickly overloaded. They often tipped over. Mounds of spilled dirt had to be scooped up. The tracks required frequent readjustment. Digging stopped often. Workers cleaned

up spills and moved train tracks. The project was not moving along fast enough. Wallace needed a new plan.

To compound his troubles, an illness attacked his crew: yellow fever. Victims of the disease showed severe symptoms. These included bleeding gums and black vomit. Yellow fever often resulted in death. Workers were afraid of catching the disease. Five hundred American workers fled the Canal Zone. Wallace soon followed. After just one year of work, the United States was also about to fail at building the canal.

A New Leader

Roosevelt refused to give up on his dream. He immediately called upon railroad company leader John Stevens to head the project. Stevens was familiar with large engineering projects. He was a main leader in the construction of the Great Northern Railway that crossed the Pacific Northwest.

Stevens approached the canal project with a new plan. He organized a machine park. Equipment could be stored there and be ready throughout the canal project. Stevens also realized that the railroad would serve as the backbone of the entire project. He knew that the railroad would carry resources in and out of the Canal Zone. He also knew that the railroad would be the most effective way to move dirt and rocks out of digging zones.

Stevens's knowledge of rail systems was helpful. He quickly set out to improve the railway that served the Canal Zone. Stevens ordered the tracks to be upgraded. He installed heavier, double tracks. He directed workers to **reinforce** bridges. Stevens increased the rail fleet. He ordered heavier freight cars, dump cars, and **locomotives**.

Moving the Dirt

One of Stevens's biggest accomplishments was the creation of a new type of rail system. The new system was made to remove spoil. Stevens, along with William Bierd, engineered a special type of train track. The new track could remain in one piece while being lifted from the ground.

The tracks could be moved from one location to another without being taken apart. A large crane, called a rail lifter, hooked to the track. The rail lifter could lift the rails and move them closer to active steam shovels. Fewer than a dozen men were needed to move a mile of track in one day. Without the use of the rail lifter, 600 men would be needed to accomplish the same task.

Moving the rails allowed steam shovels to dig and load the spoil onto train cars without having to stop to wait while the train and tracks were moved.

Workers move the specially designed train track that could be lifted and placed in another location intact.

The Culebra Cut

A complicated system of rail was laid at the most difficult excavation point, a **gorge** known as the Culebra Cut. This area consisted of enormous rocks. These rocks needed to be removed. More than 200 miles (322km) of track were laid in the 9-mile (14.5km) gorge. At the busiest times, 115 locomotives pulled more than 2,300 spoil cars loaded with dirt and rock.

No time was wasted. The steam shovels could dig without stopping. Trains could remove spoil without interrupting the stream of work. At the peak of digging, a new train was filled with spoil nearly every two minutes.

Working Conditions

John Stevens cared about the men working on the Panama Canal. Stevens improved living conditions for the workers. To raise the quality of life in the Canal Zone, Stevens ordered the construction of new housing. This housing included indoor plumbing and a proper sewage system. Refrigerated food cars were brought to the Canal Zone so workers could receive fresh food. Stevens even established clubs and restaurants so workers could relax and recharge after a long workday.

Before a shovel was used John Stevens made sure the workers living and working conditions were improved.

Dirt trains carried the spoil out of the digging location immediately. The train worked like a huge conveyor belt. Train cars were designed with sides that dropped down. A large blade, similar to a snowplow's, quickly and easily pushed the dirt off the car. Unloading an entire train of dirt took about ten minutes. The French method of using men with shovels to unload the cars required a workforce of more than 300.

Every machine used in the Culebra Cut was on rails. Steam shovels were made to move along the rails. Workers moved quickly to build new tracks in front of the steam shovels. The track left behind was taken apart and reused.

Disaster Strikes

With this system in place, the Panama Canal Project moved ahead. Stevens was proving himself to be the best man for the job. The Panama Canal was finally more than just a dream. Completion of the canal was becoming a reality.

Stevens had ordered digging to start from both ends of the canal. This plan allowed rail cars to move uphill while empty and downhill when full. By using gravity to assist the moving of spoil,

energy was conserved. The digging process moved along quickly. Americans dug more in one day than the French had managed to achieve in one month. At this rate it seemed like nothing could stop the progress.

Unfortunately for Stevens and the project, what technology was able to do, nature was able to undo. Yellow fever began to sweep through the area once again. As more workers died, the canal's completion was threatened. Stevens knew he needed help to conquer yellow fever. Dr. William Gorgas was assigned to put an end to the often deadly illness. In 1906 about 26,000 people worked on the Panama Canal. That same year, the deadly disease infected more than 21,000 workers.

A loaded train removes dirt from the Culebra Cut. Wallace had every machine used in the Culebra Cut excavation connected by rail. Loading an entire train with dirt took ten minutes. This sped up the process significantly.

Conquering the Mosquito

Old folktales had convinced many people that yellow fever was caused by a curse or spell. Many doctors believed swamp gases caused the illness. But Gorgas had a different idea about what caused yellow fever.

While living in Cuba, Gorgas had studied a similar disease called malaria.

Malaria was carried by mosquitoes. Gorgas believed that mosquitoes also spread yellow fever. Being a man with a military background, Gorgas developed a plan to attack and defeat the disease. He set out to get rid of the insect that spread it.

Yellow Fever

Yellow fever threatened the progress of the Panama Canal. The symptoms were frightening and caused many workers to flee the Canal Zone. There is no cure for yellow fever, so victims can only hope they are strong enough to survive the disease.

The illness has two phases. During the first phase, symptoms are similar to those of the common flu. Victims experience headaches, shivers, nausea, muscle aches, vomiting, and fever. If the disease moves to the second phase, terrifying symptoms take hold. High fever returns, causing liver trauma and jaundice, or yellowing of the skin. Bleeding can occur from the mouth, nose, eyes, and stomach. Blood is often noticed in the patient's vomit. At this stage many experience kidney failure and death.

Gorgas used military accuracy and force. Because mosquitoes breed and develop in water, crews sprayed oil over areas of standing water. Crews of more than 4,000 men sprayed ditches, ponds, and puddles. Horse-drawn wagons pulled tanks filled with oil. Long pipes extended from the tanks, and oil oozed out from holes in the pipes. As the oil spread over the standing water, it suffocated the mosquito larva.

Every step was taken to eliminate mosquitoes. Netting, sprays, and screens were used to keep mosquitoes away from people. By 1906 cases of yellow fever had dropped by half. Six months later the disease was completely wiped out. Gorgas had proved that mosquitoes were responsible for spreading yellow fever. Not only did he discover how to stop a

Dr. William Gorgas supervises water removal efforts at a canal site. Gorgas put together an aggressive plan for mosquito removal.

disease, he saved the Panama Canal project.

A New Threat

With the threat of yellow fever out of the way, canal construction could start again. Progress returned at a wild pace. More than 400,000 pounds (181,437kg) of dynamite, or TNT, was used each month. Workers used TNT to blast away rock and earth. Most of the blasting occurred at the Culebra Cut. But other challenges followed.

In May 1906 the Chagres River unleashed its power. During a particularly heavy storm, showers dropped more than 5 inches (12.7cm) of water per hour. The river rose above its banks. Swift, wild floodwaters tore through the Canal Zone. When the water first rolled over the river's banks, it flowed at a rate of 8,200 cubic feet (232 cubic meters)

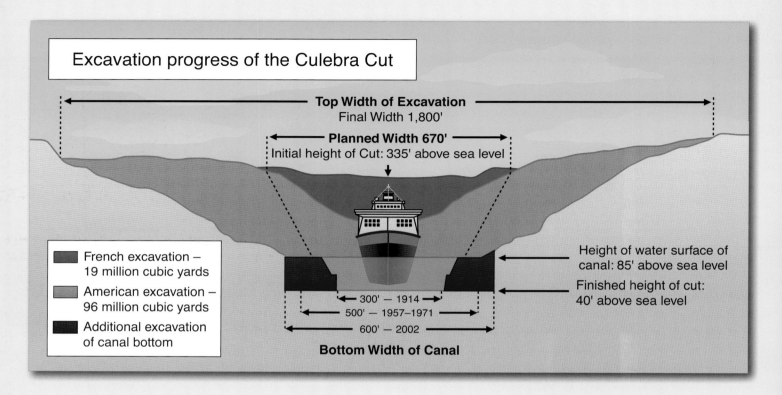

Excavation progress of the Culebra Cut

Top Width of Excavation
Final Width 1,800'

Planned Width 670'
Initial height of Cut: 335' above sea level

French excavation –
19 million cubic yards

American excavation –
96 million cubic yards

Additional excavation
of canal bottom

Height of water surface of
canal: 85' above sea level

Finished height of cut:
40' above sea level

300' — 1914
500' — 1957–1971
600' — 2002

Bottom Width of Canal

per second. At the peak of the flood, water flowed at a rate of 90,000 cubic feet (2,549 cubic meters) per second.

The flood washed away much of the digging progress. Mud slides filled in large areas. Faced with digging out af-

ter the flood and knowing he had to blast through more than 300 feet (91m) of rock across a 9-mile (14.5) span, Stevens realized the plan to dig a canal at sea level was simply impossible.

Chapter 3

A New Plan

The plan to create a sea level canal ended with the flood of 1906. But the dream to build the Panama Canal was still alive. A new idea was introduced. Rather than send ships sailing through a canal dug through the land like a river, ships would be lifted up and over the mountains at Culebra. The technology to achieve this great task was already in use. Locks, or water elevators, were the solution to the problem.

Did You Know?

Richard Halliburton, who swam the Panama Canal in 1928, paid the lowest toll. It cost him 36 cents to cross through the canal.

Locks are mechanized waterways. They act as water elevators to raise and lower ships. The plan to use locks included the formation of a new path for the canal. The new path required a new construction plan. The mighty Chagres River

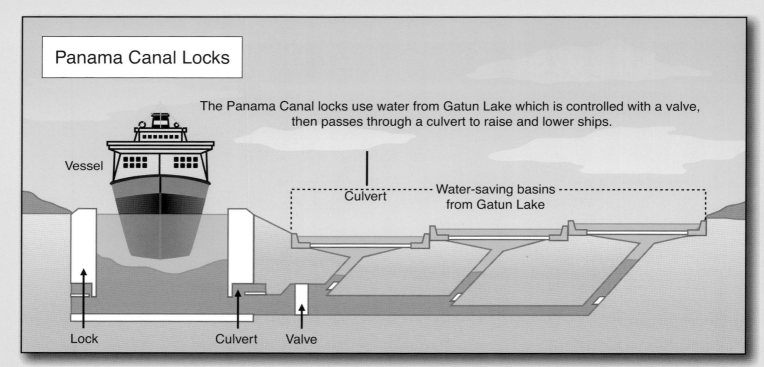

Panama Canal Locks

The Panama Canal locks use water from Gatun Lake which is controlled with a valve, then passes through a culvert to raise and lower ships.

Vessel

Culvert

Water-saving basins
from Gatun Lake

Lock   Culvert   Valve

would be dammed. The dam would flood the surrounding area, forming Gatun Lake, then the largest human-made lake on earth. Giant sets of locks would raise ships from the Pacific Ocean up to Gatun Lake. Ships would pass through the lake and carefully navigate the Culebra Cut.

A second set of locks would lower ships back down to sea level and send them into the Atlantic Ocean.

Moving Forward

Just as a new plan was put in place, Stevens quit the canal project. His leave

Colonel George Goethals took over leadership from Stevens and quickly became a master at coordinating workers and machines.

was sudden and without explanation. In 1907 a new leader was assigned to the project. Roosevelt chose Colonel George Goethals. As a military man, Goethals was under direct control of the US government. He was not allowed to quit or leave his post.

Goethals set to work. In 1907 crews began to build an earthen dam across the Chagres River. The dam was more than

1.5 miles (2.4km) wide. It was topped by a concrete spillway. The spillway would redirect water if it ever reached the top of the dam. The Chagres dam flooded the

Roosevelt Medals

President Theodore Roosevelt wanted to create a special medal to thank workers for their dedication and effort in building the Panama Canal. Leftover French machinery was collected, melted, and used to cast the medals. Canal medals were only awarded to US citizens. Each medal was given a unique number. The designs varied according to the reason for the award. Today, the medals are collected and can cost anywhere from $350 to $3,000.

Tens of thousands of men worked under Goethals to create the canal. Millions of pounds of TNT were used. Many miles of train tracks were used by hundreds of locomotives. Goethals made sure that work progressed smoothly and efficiently. Goethals used a map to plot every drill, every locomotive, and every steam shovel.

Careful calculations were made each day. Accurate numbers helped Goethals plan how long each task would take. Every man on the crew followed a detailed schedule. The entire operation was choreographed as carefully as a ballet. Men in tall towers at the cut observed construction traffic. They gave directions to workers below. Yardmasters gave directions

river and created Gatun Lake. Gatun Lake covers a 164-square-mile (425 square kilometer) area. The lake is an important section of the Canal Zone. Ships use it as part of the journey through the canal.

Gatun Lake

After the Chagres River dam was completed, the flooding that resulted created the largest human-made lake of its day. Today, Gatun Lake hosts an abundant assortment of wildlife. Gatun Lake is home to large crocodiles, tarpon, and caiman. The lake contains many islands. Before the dam flooded the Chagres River, these islands were hills. Many animal species live on the islands. Examples include the jaguar, puma, ocelot, and jacarundi. The area is also home to more than 400 species of birds.

Lake Gatun is part of the Panama Canal system.

to locomotive drivers. Workers did not have to question what to do or when to do it. Communication was efficient. As long as everyone followed the plan, operations moved forward and progress was made.

Challenges in the Culebra Cut

Goethals had mastered coordinating workers and machines. Controlling Mother Nature was a different problem. Even with the Chagres River controlled by a dam, mud slides and rock slides plagued men working in the Culebra Cut. Gravity played against the workers. The steep angles of the cliffs sent rocks and dirt sliding to the bottom of the canyon. Landslides became so serious that nearby homes and neighborhoods were pulled down to the bottom of the cut.

Workers covered the cliffs with concrete. They hoped the concrete would seal the earth and stop the landslides. The idea was not successful. The concrete simply crumbled down the cliff when the next slide occurred. So workers tried another idea. They excavated from the top of the cut down. They hoped that decreasing the weight at the top of the cut would result in fewer slides. But the landslides continued.

The only solution to the problem involved a balance of gravity. The angle of the cliff was too steep. Gravity kept pulling more earth downward. Workers had to keep cutting away at the cliff until they reached an angle that would not trigger another slide, but the process took time and proved to be dangerous. On January 19, 1912, a devastating slide completely filled the cut from one side to the other. Frustrated workers looked to their leader, Goethals. He replied by giving simple instructions and told crews all they could do was dig it out again.

Through the course of the canal's construction, more than 61 million pounds (28 million kg) of TNT was used to blast away mountain rock. For seven years the Culebra Cut boomed with dynamite blasts. Twenty-four hours a day, seven days a week, workers moved rock to make way for the locks. They worked to widen the passage that would allow ships to travel from one ocean to the other.

SS Ancon

The SS *Ancon* was more than just a ceremonial vessel. It was a steamship that played an important role in the construction of the Panama Canal. The ship was purchased by the Panama Railway Company and put to work. The ship was used to bring workers and supplies into the Canal Zone. It was most helpful in transporting tons of cement that was used in the construction of the locks. The *Ancon* was honored upon the canal's completion. On August 15, 1914, during a ceremonial opening, the *Ancon* was the first ship to officially transit the canal.

Building the Locks

While some workers battled the cut, others began to work on the locks. Construction of the locks started in 1909. More than 48,000 men were assigned to

concrete with every load. As the buckets were dumped, workers stomped through knee-deep concrete to spread it into the right places. A continuous supply of buckets traveled on cables through the air. Each bucket zipped along at about 20 miles per hour (32kph). Delivery of concrete to the lock chambers was quick and efficient.

the lock project. Building the locks took four years.

During construction, concrete was carried to the locks in large buckets. The buckets were suspended by a system of cables. Each bucket carried 6 tons (5.4t) of

The locks were constructed in 36-foot (11m) sections. Each section took about a week to complete. More than 5 million bags of cement were used to create the locks. After observing the workers who dumped the bags of concrete, Goethals had an idea. One simple instruction saved the project a great deal of money. He ordered workers to shake the sacks after dumping them out. The amount of concrete recovered from the bottom of the bags saved the project more than $50,000.

Each end of the canal contains a double set of locks. Double locks allow ships to pass simultaneously in each direction. The pass at Pedro Miguel contains one pair of locks, Miraflores consists of two pair, and the locks at Gatun contain three pairs. In all, the Panama Canal consists

Did You Know?

When canal traffic is heavy, ships can pay extra money to jump ahead in line. An oil tanker once paid $220,300 to move to the front of the line.

of twelve lock chambers. The floor of each chamber is made up of at least 13 feet (4m) of solid concrete.

Each lock chamber is larger than the RMS *Titanic*. Great steel gates seal the ends of the chambers. The steel gates are hollow, which makes them light enough to float. By floating, the gates require less energy to open and close. The walls of each lock chamber are 81 feet (25m) tall and 1,000 feet (305m) long. Their length is only 250 feet (76m) shorter than the Empire State Building.

The locks are engineered to function with the assistance of gravity. Just as an elevator lifts people and cargo, the locks lift ships. Giant pipes under each lock allow water to surge into the chamber from a higher-level water supply; either Gatun Lake or Miraflores Lake. The buoyant, steel gates close and trap the water inside each chamber. As the water rushes in, the ship rises. When the ship rises to the proper level, locomotives, called mules, move ships to the next cell. Valves are opened and water flows into the next cell. Once again the ship rises to the next level. The process repeats itself until each ship is raised 85 feet (26m), high enough to meet Gatun Lake. Ships sail across Gatun Lake, then repeat the process. This time the process works in reverse. Each lock chamber lowers the vessel to sea level. Finally, the ship is released into the ocean.

The Dream Becomes a Reality

In 1913 construction was nearly complete. The final earthen dam was removed. Water filled the last dry construction areas. The dream of completing the Panama Canal had finally been realized. During a ceremonial dedication, the cargo ship SS *Ancon* made the maiden voyage through the Panama Canal. The face of the earth had been changed, and ship travel would never again be the same.

A production line of industrial cement mixers used over 5 million bags of cement in the construction of the locks.

A New World

The opening of the Panama Canal in 1914 changed the geography and economy of the world. It placed a new divide through a continent. It changed the shipping industry. Sailing around the southern tip of South America once took four weeks. Now ships sail through the canal in about ten hours. Over the course of the fourteen-year project, the United States spent $375 million. That amount would equal over 8 billion of today's dollars. A total of 56,307 workers from the United States, the West Indies, and Europe created an engineering marvel.

For a century, the canal has served as the shipping shortcut of the world. In

1914, 1,000 ships passed through during the entire year. Today, more than 14,000 ships of all sizes sail through the canal annually. More than 30 ships pass through the canal each day. An estimated 200 million pieces of cargo are carried through the canal each year. Each ship that passes through the canal must pay a fee called a toll. In 2012 the Panama Canal Authority generated more than $800 million in profits from tolls. The canal is an important part of Panama's economy and greatly influences the world economy.

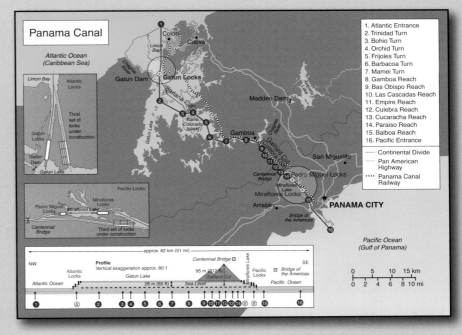

Maintaining the Canal

Planning and hard work keep the canal operating smoothly. The Culebra Cut sits over two tectonic plates, separate sections of the earth's crust. When these plates move, mud slides and rock slides send spoil into the cut. Millions of tons of earth fall into the cut each year. Workers use **dredging** machines to keep the cut clean. If they did not remove the fallen rocks and mud, the cut would become

Over 14,000 ships use the canal annually.

too shallow. Ships could no longer pass through. Dredging machines remove more dirt during annual maintenance than did the original workers who built the canal.

Maintaining the canal is a big project. Repairing mechanical equipment is a big job. Ship traffic is so heavy that it is hard to schedule lock repairs. The Panama Canal never closes, so workers must try to make repairs between ship passings.

Most large maintenance projects are planned for late-night hours, when ship traffic is slow. A 23-story floating crane, called the Titan, is used to change the lock gates. Each lock gate weighs as much as almost 4,000 jet airliners. The Titan lifts each gate up to its location in the lock cell. Underwater, a robotic camera sends images to a worker. Called a controller, the worker maneuvers the replacement gate into place. Removing, fixing, and returning lock gates is an expensive task. Well-trained experts must control the job.

Getting a Panamax Through the Canal

Helping ships pass through the canal also requires workers who are highly trained. Ships today are very large and filled with goods. A small mistake can result in an accident. That can mean a large sum of money being lost.

Cargo ships are changing. Builders are making them larger and larger. The largest ship that can pass through the Panama Canal is called a Panamax. A Panamax must pay about $250,000 in tolls for passage through the Panama Canal.

Panama Canal officials say the high cost is necessary. A Panamax ship

Panama Canal Treaty

On September 7, 1977, President Jimmy Carter signed the Panama Canal Treaty. The treaty stated that control of the canal would be given to the Panamanians by the year 2000. Before that, the canal was both built and controlled by the United States.

requires three pilots to pass through the canal. Each pilot must take an eight-year training course before being certified to navigate a ship through the canal.

The process of moving a Panamax ship through the canal is complicated. First, rowboats use ropes to attach each ship to the lock chamber walls. Next, powerful and specialized rail cars, called mules,

The Panamax (pictured) is the largest ship that can pass through the canal.

ship rises up as the water rushes into the lock. It takes only eight minutes for the ship to move up three stories.

Expanding the Canal

Canal officials use modern technology to keep equipment and ships running smoothly. Computers with a global positioning system and maritime tracking software are helpful. These tools tell pilots exactly where each ship is at all times. **Collisions** of large ships are a constant threat. Pilots and canal workers must be very careful. Panamax ships carry millions of dollars of cargo. A collision would cost many people a great deal of money. An accident could cause people to get hurt.

pull the ship into the lock. Each mule can pull up to 35 tons (32t). It takes eight mules to pull a Panamax ship. A Panamax ship squeezes into the lock chamber with only inches to spare. Once inside the lock chamber, the chamber gates close. One hundred valves at the bottom of the chamber open, letting water rush in. It takes 25,888,861 gallons (98,000,000L) to fill one lock chamber. The Panamax

The Panama Canal is a big economic influence. It saves time for shipping companies, which means they save money as well. Panama makes money by collecting tolls. In today's world, economic factors are changing. Shipbuilders are creating ships that are even larger than the Panamax vessels. Larger vessels are able to carry more goods. The Panama Canal must keep up with the demands of the shipping industry. If Panama cannot keep up, shipping companies may look for new options to deliver goods.

To modernize the canal, a $5 billion expansion plan is under way. Workers are adding a new set of locks to the canal. The locks will allow ships nearly twice the size of Panamax ships to pass through. Newly designed lock gates are being installed. The new gates roll side to side on tracks, rather than swinging back and forth on pins. The new gates are being constructed from special concrete blocks that are hollow. The special blocks cut down on the weight of the gates so much that a small trolley will be used to open and close them. The new gates will require less maintenance and they will be easier to replace. The new design makes operation of the canal more efficient.

Panama Canal Tugboats

Tugboats play an important role at the Panama Canal. They help keep ships safe. Tugboats direct ships as they pass through the canal and stick with them until they reach the opposite end. Tugboats can help a ship if it loses power or if it should happen to drift toward another large ship. Because large ships are so hard to steer and maneuver, they rely on tugboats to help them travel through the canal.

A tugboat leads a container ship as it leaves the Miraflores Locks. Tugs help ships steer through the canal.

On the Cutting Edge

The expansion plan also includes steps to widen and deepen the Culebra Cut. Larger ships will pass through the locks. These ships will need more room to pass through the cut. Larger ships are harder to control. So engineers are working to straighten the path through the cut.

Workers are using explosives to remove the curves in the cut. A giant, floating barge is used for this work. The drill barge, called the *Baroo*, is larger than two tennis courts. It is used to drill holes 82 feet (25m) underwater. The holes sink 30 feet (9m) into the rock at the bottom of the canal. Each hole is filled with explosives. Once about

40 holes are drilled, they are packed with explosives. The explosives are set off. Water, mud, and rocks fly into the air. Each blast helps to straighten the cut.

To widen the cut, machine workers use a machine called the Christianson. The Christianson is a massive dredge shovel. It can lift the weight of eight buses in one scoop. Sometimes the Christianson scoops up large boulders. Care is taken to blow up the large rocks. If left alone, these large boulders could shift and roll into the path of a ship. The sharp edges could rip the sides of a ship wide open, causing the vessel to sink.

The total cost of the Panama Canal expansion project is estimated to reach $5.25 billion. The expansion project puts the Panama Canal at the cutting edge of transportation, allowing amazing feats to be achieved each day.

Glossary

collisions [co-LIZ-yuns]: Instances of an object coming into contact with another object in a violent manner.

dredging [DREDJ-ing]: Digging up or removing earth by means of a scoop or shovel, frequently at the bottom of a river or body of water.

excavators [EX-ca-vay-tors]: Workers who use a machine designed to dig or transport dirt, rock, or other forms of earth.

gorge [GORJ]: A narrow canyon with steep cliffs or walls, frequently having a running stream or river at its base.

isthmus [ISTH-mus]: A narrow strip of land, surrounded by water on two sides, that connects two larger areas of land.

locomotives [lo-ca-MOW-tives]: Moving engines that are used to push or pull a train, individual cars, or a ship.

reinforce [re-in-FORCE]: To add material in order to make stronger.

rock slides [ROCK SLIDZ]: Events where a bulk of rocks and earth detach from a cliff and are pulled down by gravity.

sea level [see LEV-el]: A level that corresponds to the sea.

spoil [SPOYL]: Waste material that is produced during digging, excavating, or blasting.

yellow fever [YELL-o FEE-ver]: An infectious and often deadly disease most prominent in tropical regions.

For More Information

Books

William Fria
Portrait of the Panama Canal: From Construction to the Twenty-First Century. Portland, OR: Graphic Arts, 2011.

Ulrich Keller
The Building of the Panama Canal in Historic Photographs. New York: Dover, 1983.

David McCullough
The Path Between the Seas: The Creation of the Panama Canal, 1870–1914. New York: Simon and Schuster, 1977.

Matthew Parker
Panama Fever: The Epic Story of the Building of the Panama Canal. New York: Random House, 2009.

Websites

The American Experience:
Panama Canal
www.pbs.org/wgbh/americanexperience/
films/panama

Canal de Panamá
www.pancanal.com

Canal Museum.com
www.canalmuseum.com

History.com, Panama Canal Locks
www.history.com/videos/panama-canal-locks

Panama Canal Museum
www.panamacanalmuseum.org

Index

B
Balboa, Vasco Núñez de, 7
Baroo (drill barge), 42
Bucyrus steam shovel, 14

C
Canal Zone, U.S. control
  over, 10
Cape Horn, 4–5, 6, *6*
Carter, Jimmy, 39
Cement mixers, *35*
Chagres River, 9, *9*, 23–24
  damming of, 25–26, 27–30
Charles I (king of Spain), 4
Christianson (dredge shovel),
  43
Construction, 14
  completion of, 34

in expansion of canal,
  41–43
of locks, *32*, 32–33, 43
of railroad, 15–17
setbacks in, 14–17
Culebra (Gaillard) Cut, 18–
  20, *21*, 23, *24*, 25, 42
challenges in, 30–32
excavation of, *24*

G
Gaillard Cut. See Culebra Cut
Gatun Lake, 28, *29*, 34
Goethals, George, 27, *27*, 28,
  30–31
Gorgas, William, 20–23, *23*

H
Halliburton, Richard, 25

I
Isthmus of Panama, 7, *7*, 8

L
Locks, 25, *26*, *32*, 31–34, 36
  construction of, *32*, 31–34,
  43

P
Panama Canal
  control of 10, 37
  expansion of, 40–43
  French work on, 11–12, *12*
  maintenance of, 37–39
  opening of, 36
  See also Construction
Panama Canal Treaty (1977),
  39
Panamax ships, 39–40, *40*, 41

About the Author

Heather Miller works as an author, artist, and teacher in northeast Indiana. She writes books for young readers and articles for an arts magazine in her hometown. She enjoys meeting interesting people who think creatively, and she spends time reading about science and learning how the world works.